Lisa Leftover

Story by Sally Odgers
Illustrations by Tom Jellett

THOMSON
™
NELSON

PM Extras Chapter Books in Ruby Level Set A
Mozart
Pegasus
Lisa Leftover
Scuba Kid
The Flower Necklace
Train Music

PM Extras Chapter Books
Ruby Level Set A

The PM Library is published by Thomson Learning Australia and is distributed as follows:

AUSTRALIA
102 Dodds Street
Southbank 3006
Victoria

NEW ZEALAND
Nelson Price Milburn
1 Te Puni Street
Petone

First published in 2004
10 9 8 7 6 5 4 3 2 1
07 06 05 04

Text © Nelson Australia Pty Limited 2004
Illustrations © Nelson Australia Pty Limited 2004

Lisa Leftover
    ISBN 0 17 011462 7
    ISBN 0 17 011457 0 (set)

Illustrations by Tom Jellett
Edited by Angelique Campbell-Muir
Designed by Leigh Ashforth
Typeset in Plantin
Printed in China by Midas Printing (Asia) Ltd

Nelson Australia Pty Limited ACN 058 280 149 (incorporated in Victoria)
trading as Thomson Learning Australia.

Contents

CHAPTER 1

Goodbye Marina

Marina was leaving.

Every time Lisa thought about it she felt cold inside. Marina had always lived next door. And for as long as she could remember, Lisa had spent as much time at Marina's place as she had at her own.

Marina couldn't go away. It would be the same as Mum going away. Or Dad.

'You *can't* go away!' Lisa had said, desperately. 'This is where you live.'

'That's what I told Mum,' said Marina. 'But she says we have to go.' Marina looked like a ruffled ginger cat. Not a bit like the cheerful best friend Lisa knew.

Marina was the ideas person. She was the one who started things up and got things moving. Life was never dull with Marina living next door.

And now Marina was leaving.

'You'll soon make new friends,' said Mum as the big moving van lumbered away from the house next door. She gently squeezed Lisa's shoulder.

Lisa didn't answer. She was too miserable to even think about making new friends.

CHAPTER 2

How Do You 'Make' a Friend?

It was horrible after Marina had gone. Suddenly, there was no one to laugh with, and no one to brighten wet weekends. Worst of all, there was no one to sit with at lunchtime or to match up with when Ms Gleeson said, 'Get into pairs.'

'Everyone else is already half of a pair,' said Lisa. 'There are nineteen people in our class now that Marina's not here. I'm the one left over.'

Ms Gleeson tried putting them into threes, but that still left Lisa on her own. Lisa Leftover.

'You can be *my* partner,' said Ms Gleeson.

That was all right in class, but what good was it in the playground? Ms Gleeson didn't skip backwards or practise Martian karate moves or hunt invisible dinosaurs as Marina had done.

'There are other fish in the sea,' said Mum. 'I'm sure you could make friends with some of the others – there are plenty of kids in your class. What about Kaitlin? She's a nice girl.'

Kaitlin *was* a nice girl. She was friendly and popular. But she already had a best friend – Dan.

'That doesn't matter,' said Mum when Lisa pointed this out. 'It's good to have more than one friend.'

'But how do you *make* friends with someone you know already?'

'Just be friendly,' said Mum. 'Just go up and talk to her.'

The next day, Lisa decided to follow her mum's advice and walked up to Kaitlin and Dan in the playground. They were talking exitedly about the latest episode of *City Café*.

'Wasn't it cool when Ali came in and Tiana tipped coffee over his head!' Dan was saying.

'And then she found out it wasn't Ali who had painted the picture at all.' Kaitlin said. 'It was Tom, um...?'

'Tom Palliser,' finished Dan. 'Rob Kitchener. Remember, he was in *Loop the Loop* last year.'

Lisa frowned. She had seen bits of *City Café* now and then, but what was *Loop the Loop*? Lisa had no idea what Kaitlin and Dan were talking about. How could she be friends with people she couldn't even have a conversation with?

Marina didn't think much of TV. She always said she'd rather do things herself than watch other people doing them. Lisa thought so too.

Lisa hovered next to the other girls until Kaitlin glanced at her again. 'Hey, Lisa. Did you see the bit when Ali came in and Tiana tipped coffee on him?'

Lisa shook her head.

'Oh. Well, then, did you see it on Monday? Tom Palliser thought someone was trying to steal...'

Lisa shook her head again. 'I don't watch *City Café*,' she said.

'Oh,' said Kaitlin. 'It's no good trying to explain it to you then.' She turned back to Dan.

Lisa hovered for a bit longer, and then walked away. Kaitlin and Dan were best friends. She was just Lisa Leftover.

CHAPTER 3

Football Fever

'What about Emily?' suggested Mum. 'You went to her house a few weeks ago.'

'But Marina was with me.'

'Well, Emily asked you as well. I'll give her mum a ring.'

'No!' said Lisa in horror. But Mum did it anyway.

'Emily's mum has invited us to the football on Saturday,' she said after hanging up. 'How's that?'

'But we *never* go to the football!' protested Lisa.

'Then maybe it's time we did,' said Mum.

If Kaitlin knew all about TV shows, then Emily knew all about sport. She could tell you which team had won the Premiership for the past five years.

Emily grinned brightly when Lisa and Mum met her at the gate of the oval. 'Ma's gone ahead with Kev to save us some seats,' she said. 'C'mon!'

They followed Emily through cheerful crowds and up into the grandstand. Suddenly, a roar went up and hundreds of people surged to their feet.

'What—' began Lisa.

'The home team has just come out,' said Mum, pointing to the players running out onto the ground. She pressed Lisa into the seat next to Emily. 'The game's about to start.'

Emily certainly enjoyed the game. She cheered and booed and waved her scarf, and yelled encouragement to her favourite players.

Lisa sat beside her and felt as if she had wandered into a foreign country by mistake.

At half time, Emily turned to her and beamed. 'It's great, isn't it? That goal of Perry's...'

'Who?'

'Perry Lockhardt, you know, number 5?'

But Lisa didn't know. She knew all the rules to 'Cornerball', a game Marina had invented, but she'd certainly never heard of anyone called Perry Lockhardt.

After the game, Emily queued to get an autograph from her favourite player. Lisa queued behind her and felt like a fraud.

Emily was a proper football fan. She was just Lisa Leftover.

CHAPTER 4

Twenty Again

Lisa did try hard to make new friends. She went to the end-of-term Dance Party with Jodette and Kim, and to the go-kart track with Izzie and Geri. The others didn't try to leave her out of things, but she could tell they would have had just as good a time if she hadn't been with them. Better, probably, since she didn't know the latest tunes and had never been in a go kart before.

And when Lisa wasn't confused, she was bored. And she always felt left over.

It was no use pretending. She had never been bored or confused with Marina. She had never been Lisa Leftover before Marina went away.

The holidays seemed to last forever.

Then, at the beginning of the next term, a new girl came to the school. Her name was Pen Smith, and she seemed as plain and simple as her name. She had straight, no-bounce hair, dark chocolate eyes and teeth like a friendly rabbit.

Pen's arrival brought the class numbers up to twenty again.

'Lisa Liffey will look after you, Pen,' said Ms Gleeson brightly on the first day.

Lisa sighed. Of course, Lisa Leftover would look after the new girl. Ms Gleeson obviously thought she had been very clever to arrange it.

A new friend for Lisa Leftover! That will soon stop her moping! Oh, Lisa could read Ms Gleeson's mind.

'But you can't make friends with someone just because they're there,' Lisa complained to Mum when she got home from school that afternoon.

'But it doesn't mean that you can't, either,' answered Mum. 'She might be a very nice girl, but you'll never know if you don't spend some time with her and try to find out.'

'Pen's okay, but she's *so* quiet,' Lisa protested.

'There's nothing wrong with being quiet,' said Mum.

'But she just sits there. She never *does* anything.'

'That's because she doesn't know anyone, so she doesn't have anyone to do things with,' said Mum.

Lisa sighed. She decided it was no use trying to explain it to Mum.

The next day, they had both finished their contract work, so they had free time. If Marina had been there, she would have suggested drawing a magic island, or building a staggering tower with the topple-blocks. Or inventing the recipe for a new and incredible cake. But Marina wasn't there. Only Pen was, and Pen suggested nothing.

Sighing again, Lisa took out her pencils and began to draw a magic island. *Pirates' Cove*, she wrote in tiny letters. *Fountain Mountain.*

Pen glanced sideways, and Lisa moved her arm to shield her work.

'How are you getting along with Pen?' asked Mum that afternoon when Lisa got home from school.

Lisa shrugged. 'I'm not. She's nice, and all that, but we don't have anything in common. She's so quiet. It's as if she isn't even there.'

'Not everyone talks as much as Marina,' said Mum.

Lisa just sighed.

CHAPTER 5

Silence

On Friday, Ms Gleeson's class went out for an excursion. It wasn't a bus-ride excursion, they were just walking to the park.

'This is for little kids!' Lisa thought crossly. She tucked her clipboard and pencil under her arm and headed out with everyone else. They all seemed pleased to be going out, and talked excitedly with each other.

Ms Gleeson didn't make them walk in pairs, but of course most people did. Kaitlin and Dan walked together, and so did Emily and Kev. Jodette and Kim lagged behind, and Izzie and Geri shot on ahead. As for Marcus and Rocky, they were practically out of sight before the rest of the class had even made it through the park gates.

Lisa didn't want to walk with Pen, but there was really no one else – except for Ms Gleeson. And Lisa didn't want to walk with her, either.

'Gather round!' called Ms Gleeson when they reached the huge oak tree that grew in the middle of the park.

Everyone sorted themselves out and came to stand around the oak.

'Are we going to do maypole dancing, Ms Gleeson?' asked Rocky brightly.

'No,' said Ms Gleeson. She smiled at them from under her shady hat. 'We're going to listen.'

'Huh?' Rocky stared.

'Yes,' said Ms Gleeson. 'For once you chatterboxes are going to sit quietly for five minutes and *just listen.*'

'But—'

'Ssh!' Ms Gleeson held up her finger. 'Get into pairs, make yourselves comfortable, and listen. I don't want a sound out of any one of you for the next five minutes. What I want you to do is to write down any *other* sounds you hear. And now – let's have some silence!'

CHAPTER 6

Silent Sounds

Of course, Lisa found herself paired with Pen Smith. Who else would pick Lisa Leftover when they all had best friends already?

Lisa sighed.

Silence.

It was very strange. At first, there were muffled giggles and some low-voiced conversation, but Ms Gleeson looked hard at the culprits, and soon there really was silence.

Then a bird twittered in the oak tree.

Lisa braced her clipboard against her knees and wrote. *Bird.*

Silence.

A small breeze ruffled the branches.

Rustling leaves, Lisa wrote.

Pen Smith's pencil was scratching busily, so Lisa added that, too. *Pencil lead on paper.*

But what was Pen writing? There was hardly anything to hear in the park on a weekday morning.

Lisa glanced over at Pen's clipboard and her eyes widened.

Rocky nearly bursting to talk, Pen had written. *I can hear the words trying to get out of his mouth.* And, *Ms Gleeson enjoying the silence for a change.*

Lisa opened her mouth to ask Pen if she could really hear that, but Ms Gleeson looked at her hard.

Lisa picked up her pencil again. *Lisa Leftover wondering if Pen can really hear that*, she wrote.

Silently, she passed her clipboard to Pen.

Pen read the sentence, and smiled. 'Oh, yes,' she said. Well, she mouthed the words but no sound came out of her mouth. She steadied her own clipboard and wrote, *Pen New-Girl wondering if Lisa-the-Silent really doesn't like her.*

Lisa smiled quickly, and nervously shook her head.

Pen grinned. 'Phew!' said her mouth and her expression, and she fanned herself with her hand.

Lisa caught Ms Gleeson's eye and took back her clipboard.

A dog barking in the distance, she wrote. *The sound of bees in the blossom. The silent sound of making a new friend...*

CHAPTER **7**

Smiling Lisa

'So!' said Mum brightly, when Lisa came home from school that day. 'What's happened to you?'

Lisa stared. 'What do you mean?'

'*Something's* happened,' said Mum. 'You've gone from being Lisa Leftover to Smiling Lisa, all in a single day.'

'Oh!' Lisa hadn't realised, but now Mum had pointed it out, she knew the corners of her mouth were turning up.

'I sort of made a new friend,' she said, and she told Mum about the excursion and the silence in the park.

'In one way, the park was really quiet,' she continued, 'but when I listened properly, there *were* sounds. I just hadn't noticed them before. And Pen's a lot of fun, even though she's quiet. I just hadn't noticed that before, either.'

'And now you have noticed,' said Mum. 'And noticing has cheered you up.' She waggled her finger at Lisa. 'I recommend you keep right on noticing things from now on.'

Lisa nodded agreement. 'Is it okay if Pen comes around after school tomorrow?'

'Of course,' said Mum. 'I'll look forward to meeting her. What are you two planning to do?'

'I don't really know. We haven't decided.'

'Well, what does Pen like to do?'

Lisa shrugged. 'I still don't know her very well, but I do know one thing. Getting to know her is going to be lots of fun!'